AQA A
Unit 4 Further A
Ac

By

Brendan Casey

Other Titles in this Series

AQA AS Accounting
Unit 1 Introduction to Financial Accounting
Unit 2 Financial and Management Accounting

AQA A2 Accounting
Unit 3 Further Aspects of Financial Accounting

ISBN 978 1500685201

Copyright © Brendan Casey 2016

Table of contents

Manufacturing accounts	3
Further budgeting	5
Types of costs & contribution	10
Break-even analysis	12
Marginal costing	15
Absorption costing	20
Standard costing	24
Capital investment appraisal	28
Social accounting	31
Activity Based Costing (ABC)	32
APPENDIX 1 – Manufacturing & Income statement layout and extract from Balance Sheet	34
APPENDIX 2 - Budget Layouts	36
APPENDIX 3 - Marginal cost statement	38
APPENDIX 4 – Standard Costing Reconciliation Statements	39

About the author

The author is Head of Accounting at Ashbourne Independent Sixth Form College in London, and is a graduate of the London School of Economics. He has been teaching the AQA A level accounting syllabus for over 15 years.

Aim of this book

This book is intended as a quick reference revision guide. It's particularly aimed at the written questions, which students often struggle on, but account for about 20-25% of the exam. It also contains appendices of important formats, ratios and definitions.

Manufacturing accounts

1

Manufacturing accounts are the final accounts of manufacturing businesses.

1.1 Layout

See appendix 1.

1.2 Limitations

- **Problem of classifying direct and indirect costs** – often estimates are used therefore the figure for prime costs and factory costs may be estimates as well.
- **Problem of valuing work-in-progress** – this may be difficult to measure accurately.
- **Lack of detail on the cost of individual products** – manufacturing accounts give the total cost production. They don't give any breakdown on individual products.
- **No information on efficiency** – we can't tell whether the manufacturing was done efficiently or not because we've got nothing to compare it to.
- **Transfer pricing** – this is an estimate and can be difficult for the non-accountant to understand.

1.3 What is the purpose of transfer pricing?

- To give an estimate of how much of the gross profit is due to the firm manufacturing the goods themselves instead of buying them from an outside supplier.
- It can be used by managers to make "make or buy" decisions – if the costs of manufacture are higher than the costs of supply they may as well buy in the goods instead of making them.
- It can be used to motivate manufacturing staff by encouraging them to cut costs and keep competitive with the costs of supply.
- To charge the retailing section of the business a more realistic price for the goods.

- It can be used as a basis for calculating bonuses for manufacturing staff.

1.4 Problems of transfer pricing/arguments against transfer pricing

- It can give an unrealistic view of factory profitability unless careful research is done on comparing the costs of manufacture with the costs of supply.
- It doesn't increase or decrease gross profit and involves extra effort so isn't worthwhile.
- It's difficult to understand for non-accountants – it just confuses them.

1.5 Why is it necessary to create a provision for unrealised profit (PURP)?

The provision for unrealised profit needs to be created because of the prudence concept. This states that losses need to be recognised as soon as they are anticipated but profit should not be recognised until realised. Because of transfer pricing the closing inventory has been valued at cost plus not cost and therefore contains an element of unrealised profit. Applying the prudence concept this 'profit' therefore needs to be eliminated and the value of inventory adjusted to cost.

Further budgeting

2

2.1 Definition of a budget

A budget is a short-term financial plan. Usually they are prepared for a year in advance but some budgets are prepared over a month or per quarter.

2.2 Budgetary control

This means delegating financial planning to managers. Their performance is then evaluated against the budget and corrective action taken where necessary.

2.3 Types of budget

- Cash budget
- Sales budget
- Purchases budget
- Production budget
- Labour budget
- Receivables budget
- Payables budget
- Income statement budget
- Balance sheet budget
- Master budget

2.4 Budget layouts

See appendix 2.

2.5 Purposes/benefits of budgets

To set objectives/goals - budgets help businesses set goals and targets for the coming year. It helps them to focus on what they intend to achieve, e.g. profitability, productivity and market share
Planning - budgets help managers to plan ahead, e.g. raw materials and manpower requirements

Further budgeting

Control - budgets provide a benchmark against which the actual figures can be measured. Variances can be investigated and corrective action taken, e.g. salaries too high - too much overtime being paid; interest payments too high - find alternative sources of finance.

Evaluation - budgets can be used to evaluate performance, e.g. sales staff and managers

Aids decision-making - budgets can help make better decisions, e.g. the cash budget can be used to see when the firm will be overdrawn and may need extra sources of finance.

Improves delegation – budgets help to divide up work into definite areas and give financial responsibilities to managers. This improves delegation.

Improves co-ordination & communication - as managers are clearer about their responsibilities it's easier to co-ordinate departments and communication improves.

Financial assets used more efficiently - budgets help managers allocate resources in the most efficient way, e.g. the cash budget helps to improve the management of working capital.

2.6 Drawbacks/limitations of budgets

De-motivation - targets can be set too high. Employees and managers may feel they can't achieve them and get de-motivated, e.g. sales budget.

Training – managers require training before they can use budgets. This may be costly.

Poorer decisions may be made – managers may stick to budgets too rigidly and therefore poorer decisions are made, e.g. a sales manager may refuse to increase spending on entertainment even though it might bring in more clients because he fears going over budget.

Loss of credibility – if there are lots of variances every year budgets may lose their credibility. Managers won't stick to them and complaints increase.

2.7 How cash, production, sales and labour budgets may benefit businesses

(i) Cash budget

- Can be used to identify when there will be a bank overdraft and therefore loan facilities can be arranged in advance.
- Can be used to motivate staff so that they don't overspend on expenses.

(ii) Production budget

- Can be used to work out labour and raw material requirements for next year
- Can be used to see if extra investment is required in plant and machinery so the firm can achieve its budgeted output.

(iii) Sales budget

- Can be used to motivate sales staff to reach their sales targets
- Can be used to see which staff or teams are outperforming or underperforming.

(iv) Labour budget

- Can be used to plan and control labour costs
- Can be used to work out if new staff need to be hired in order to keep to production targets
- Can be used to work out overtime and shift working requirements

2.8 Why is the production budget important?

Planning - forces businesses to plan ahead for labour and raw material needs.
Control – allows the business to control and monitor production levels. It gives supervisors and managers benchmark figures to work with.
Motivation - gives managers and workers production targets to achieve and helps motivate them.
Investment – the production budgets may highlight the need for extra investment in new plant and machinery so that production targets can be achieved.

2.9 Factors which make for effective budgeting

Careful consideration of all factors e.g. seasonal factors, timing of receipts and payments, not being over optimistic.
Monitoring and review - figures need to be monitored by staff and managers to make sure people are sticking to them. Likewise figures need to be updated regularly to make sure they don't get out of date.
Cash budget, income statement budget and balance sheet budget to be prepared as a minimum - these show liquidity,

expected performance and expected year end figures respectively. As a minimum businesses need to prepare them.
Budgeting needs to be treated as a serious exercise - otherwise the estimates won't be reliable and poor decisions will be made.

2.10 Master budget

(i) Definition

This is an income statement and balance sheet budget prepared from all the individual operational budgets, e.g. sales budget, production budget, cash budget.

(ii) Steps in preparing the master budget

- Decide aims and objectives and set the budget period
- Gather information - this comes from previous years and by interviewing managers in the various departments.
- The budget which is the 'limiting factor' is prepared first. Usually this is the sales budget or production budget because all the other figures depend on them.
- After the sales budget has been prepared (this is usually the limiting factor) the production budget is prepared next. This includes raw material costs, direct and indirect costs and production overheads.
- Departmental budgets are then prepared for each section, e.g. sales department, financial department, personnel department.
- Sales, production and departmental budgets are then amalgamated into a master budget. This is an income statement budget and balance sheet budget for the accounting period
- The master budget is then agreed and signed by the board of directors.

(iii) Benefits of a master budget

Planning – focuses managers and directors minds on the objectives for the coming year, e.g. increase profit by 10%.
Control – forecast profits can be compared with actual profits and reasons for differences can be investigated, e.g. revenue 10% lower than expected.
Motivates – it motivates senior staff and workers as they've got concrete objectives to achieve.

Further budgeting

Aids decision-making – managers and directors can see the effects of changing for example selling price, buying price or overheads on profits.

2.11 Why a bank might refuse a request for an increased overdraft facility

No security offered - banks usually require security for big overdrafts. Perhaps the company hasn't offered any.

Badly managed business – the business may be badly managed therefore the bank doesn't want to lend them any money, e.g. no budgets prepared, no business plan or problems collecting debts

Bias in the figures - the bank may be concerned that the figures are biased. In general banks prefer the figures to be prepared by a qualified accountant rather than the owner himself as he may be biased.

Types of costs & contribution

3

3.1 Types of costs

Fixed costs – these are costs which do not vary with the level of output. They always stay the same, e.g. rent, light & heat and insurance.
Variable costs – these are costs which vary directly with the level of output, e.g. direct labour, direct materials.
Semi-variable costs – these are costs which have an element of both fixed and variable costs e.g. telephone. This has a fixed element (the line rental) and a variable element (the call charges).
Direct costs – these are costs that can be identified directly with each unit of output, e.g. direct labour, raw materials.
Indirect costs – these are costs that cannot be identified directly with a unit of output, e.g. fixed costs.
Marginal costs – these are the costs of producing an extra unit of output. It's another name for the variable costs.

3.2 Contribution

(i) Definition

Contribution is the difference between the selling price and variable costs of the business. Once fixed costs are covered contribution becomes profit. It can be measured either in total or per unit.

(ii) Formulas

- Contribution per unit = selling price per unit - variable costs per unit.

- Total contribution = contribution per unit x total output

(iii) Marginal costing (contribution) statements

Format

Types of cost and contribution

	£
Revenue	X
Variable costs	(X)
Total contribution	X
Fixed costs	(X)
Profit for year	X

Advantage of marginal costing statements

Contribution is clearly identified thereby making it easier to distinguish between the effect on profit of changes in variable costs and changes in fixed costs.

Break-even analysis

4

4.1 Definition

Break-even point (BEP) is the point at which a business is making neither a profit nor a loss.

4.2 Formula

$$BEP = \frac{Fixed\ costs}{Contribution\ per\ unit}$$

4.3 Graph

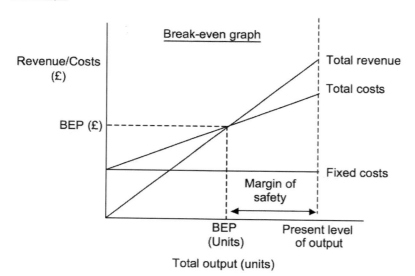

4.4 Assumptions, limitations and advantages

Assumptions

- All output is sold and there is no closing inventory.
- Linearity of data - selling price remains the same and variable costs per unit remain the same at all levels of output.

Limitations

All output will be sold – this is unlikely as most firms will keep a buffer stock.
Linearity of data – this is unlikely as competition will mean the selling price will have to be lowered at higher levels of output. Economies of scale will also mean the variable costs will decrease as output increases.
Distinction between fixed costs and variable costs – this is sometimes not easy to do and means estimates may have to be used.
Single product – break-even point analysis only works with single products. Most companies will have more than one product so it limits its usefulness.

Advantages

Shows the point at which a profit will be made - this gives a company a target to aim for and tells them the minimum number of units they need to sell to stay in business.
Aids decision-making – break-even point is an easy to understand concept. Managers can easily see the effects that changes in selling price, variable costs and fixed costs will have on the business and it therefore helps them with their decision-making.
Shows clearly the distinction between fixed costs and variable costs -
this is an important concept to grasp for managers when making decisions. Break-even point analysis is a good way of making it clear.

4.5 Advantages and disadvantages of a break-even point graph

Advantages

- It's visual – therefore it improves presentations and makes them clearer
- You can show visually the effects on break-even point of changes in selling price, variable costs and fixed costs.

Disadvantages

More difficult to get exact figures for break-even point because it may be difficult to read the scale.

4.6. Target rate of profit

Break-even analysis

This is connected with BEP. The formula is:

$$\text{No. units to achieve target profit} = \frac{\text{Fixed costs} + \text{target profit}}{\text{Contribution per unit}}$$

Marginal costing

5

5.1 Definition

Marginal costing is a costing method based on contribution. Contribution is selling price minus variable costs.

5.2 Applications

- Break-even point analysis
- Special orders
- Make or buy decisions
- Optimum use of scarce resources
- Price setting
- Competing courses of action

5.3 Special orders (one-off orders)

Special orders are one-off orders for work which fall outside normal production. If the contribution is positive the firm should accept the work. However, it needs to take into account non-financial factors as well.

Orders which give a negative contribution may still be acceptable but the circumstances would need to be exceptional, e.g. if there was a recession and the firm just wanted to keep trading in the short-run because it expected the economy to improve.

Worked example

XYZ Ltd receives a one–off order from a French retailer for 10,000 units of its product. However, it is only willing to pay £150 per unit. The normal production costs and selling price are shown below. Should it accept the order?

	£
Normal selling price	180
Direct materials	50
Direct labour	60
Fixed costs	20

Solution

Marginal costing

Contribution is £40 per unit (150-110) so in terms of financial factors the recommendation would be that the firm accepts the order. However, it also needs to take into account non-financial factors. These can be either positive or negative as shown below:

Positive

- May get repeat orders at the full price
- Opens up a new market in France
- Good for the image/reputation of the business

Negative

- Order may disrupt normal production - the firm needs to make sure it has spare capacity.
- Hidden costs, e.g. transport costs, fluctuations in the exchange rate and extra administration costs.
- Regular customers might find out and want a lower price as well.

5.4 Make or buy decisions

These are situations where the firm has to decide whether to make the product themselves or buy it in from an outside supplier.

Worked example

XYZ Ltd produces a product with selling price and costings as shown below. It's approached by a Chinese manufacturer who says they can supply the product for £30. Should they continue to make the product themselves or buy it in from the Chinese supplier?

	£
Selling price	70
Direct materials	15
Direct labour	20
Fixed costs	15

Solution

- Contribution if XYZ Ltd make the product themselves = £35 (70-35)

Marginal costing

- Contribution if XYZ Ltd buy the product from the Chinese supplier = £40 (70-30)

Based on financial factors XYZ Ltd should buy the product from the Chinese supplier. However, it also needs to take into account non-financial factors such as:

- Quality of the product
- Delivery times and reliability of the supplier
- Hidden costs, e.g. extra administration costs
- Fluctuations in the exchange rate
- Communication problems

5.5 Optimum use of scarce resources

This means situations where firms can't make all of their normal production because there is a shortage of either direct material or direct labour. We call the item there is a shortage of the limiting factor.

The technique is to rank the products in terms of contribution per limiting factor and then allocate the limiting factor to production according to the normal production pattern to find the optimal production pattern.

5.6 Price setting e.g. penetration pricing

If a business wants to gain a foothold in a new market they may adopt a marginal cost approach to pricing their product. They would be willing to sacrifice some profit in the short run to build market share. Later on once they become established they would put the price up.

Worked example

XYZ Ltd has had a great deal of success with a product in the home market. The product sells for £50. The managers want to launch the product in China. What would be the minimum price they would be willing to sell it for in order to get a foothold in the Chinese market? Costs are given below:

Variable costs per unit	£25
Fixed costs per unit	£15

Solution

Marginal costing

The minimum price would be £25, the marginal costs of production. They would of course have to take into account non-financial factors as well, e.g. a very low price might make the product look cheap which isn't the image they want.

5.7 Competing courses of action

This means trying to decide what product to produce.

Worked example

XYZ Ltd has to decide whether to produce product A, B or C. Given the information below give your recommendation.

	A £	B £	C £
Selling price per unit	500	200	300
Direct material cost per unit	120	70	90
Direct labour cost per unit	85	80	110

Total fixed costs are £35,000

Solution

	A £	B £	C £
Contribution	295	50	100

On the basis of contribution XYZ Ltd should produce product A.

5.8 Benefits/Drawbacks of marginal costing

Benefits

- Useful for decision making situations where its safe to ignore fixed costs, e.g., one-off orders, optimum use of scarce resources
- Concept of contribution easy to understand

Drawbacks

- Costs have to be identified as fixed or variable – not always easy to separate the two
- If used to work out selling price a large mark-up has to be used to take into account fixed costs. This may lead to less accurate

Marginal costing

selling prices compared to other methods, e.g. absorption costing (see 6.0), activity based costing (see 10.0).
- Not acceptable under IAS 2, inventories

Absorption costing

6

6.1 Definition

Absorption costing is the process by which fixed costs are allocated to products.

6.2 Advantages/disadvantages

Advantages

- Ensures prices are set after all costs have been considered.
- Requires thought about the best way to allocate overheads.
- Acceptable under IAS 2, inventories

Disadvantages

- Fixed costs are estimated therefore the full cost produced is only an estimated figure as well.
- The choice of basis for the OAR, e.g. machine hours, labour hours, may be arbitrary and not be relevant for all overheads, so the figures produced may lack accuracy.
- Can't be used in short-term decision-making, e.g. break-even analysis, as fixed and variable costs not separate.

6.3 Methods of allocating overheads

These are known as overhead absorption rates (OAR's). There are several of these, but the two you need to know for Unit 4 are labour hours and machine hours.

(i) Direct labour hours

Formula

$$\text{Direct labour hours rate} = \frac{\text{Total overheads}}{\text{Total direct labour hours}}$$

Used when

Absorption costing

Production is labour intensive and labour hours predominate.

(ii) Machine hours

Formula

$$\text{Machine hour rate} = \frac{\text{Total overheads}}{\text{Total machine hours}}$$

Used when

Production is capital intensive and machine hours predominate.

6.4 Evaluation of OAR's

Questions often ask you to select an appropriate OAR and justify why. The trick is to look whether labour hours or machine hours predominate in that department. If labour hours predominate it means it's a labour intensive department and you should choose that, else if machine hours predominate it means it's a machine intensive department and you should choose this instead.

6.5 Allocation and apportionment

Allocation – this means charging overheads to cost centres when those costs are easily identified as coming from that cost centre.
Apportionment - this means charging overheads to a cost centre on some rational basis, e.g. floor area, horse power, number of staff or cost of machinery.

6.6 Cost of a product

Just remember what a manufacturing account looks like.

Formula

Cost of a product = direct materials + direct labour + factory overheads

6.7 Cost centre

This is a production department, service location or item of equipment to which overhead costs can be allocated, e.g. machining, canteen or individual machines.

Absorption costing

Benefits

- Instills a sense of cost consciousness in the workforce - cuts waste.
- Improves communication, co-ordination and delegation - managers given a budget and specific roles and responsibilities.

6.8 Over and under absorption of overhead

This happens because when we allocate overheads we are using estimated figures not actual figures. The actual figures can be higher or lower giving rise to a difference.

Over-absorption of overhead - this occurs when the actual overhead is lower than the budgeted overhead.
Under-absorption of overhead - this occurs when the actual overhead is higher than the budgeted overhead.

6.9 Apportionment of overheads from reciprocal service departments

Reciprocal service departments are those that both provide a service to a production department and use that production department as well, e.g. catering is a service department that provides canteen facilities for maintenance engineers but at the same time it will need to use those maintenance engineers when there is a breakdown in machinery. In this situation we use the elimination method to allocate overheads.

Worked example

XYZ Ltd has three production departments (A, B and C) and two service departments (X and Y). Estimated overhead costs have been allocated and apportioned to each department as follows:

	Production departments			Service departments	
	A	B	C	X	Y
	£	£	£	£	£
Estimated overheads	40,000	15,000	20,000	10,000	20,000

The service departments' overheads are to be apportioned as follows:

	A	B	C	X	Y
Department X	40%	40%	10%	-	10%
Department Y	50%	30%	15%	5%	-

Solution

Absorption costing

Using the elimination method we allocate the overheads of the service department with the largest overheads first (in this case service department Y). We then allocate the overheads from the other service departments (in this case service department X). Although there is still a residual amount of overhead left in service department Y we can ignore it because it's not material and it's only an estimated figure anyway. See below.

	Production departments			Service departments	
	A	B	C	X	Y
	£	£	£	£	£
Estimated overheads	40,000	15,000	20,000	10,000	20,000
Department Y	10,000	6,000	3,000	1,000	-
Department X	4,400	4,400	1,100	(11,000)	1,100
Total overheads	54,400	25,400	24,100		

6.10 Calculation of profit using absorption and marginal costing

The biggest difference to remember is that when valuing closing inventory absorption costing includes all costs, including fixed costs, but marginal costing only uses variable costs. Because of this the closing inventory is higher, and profits higher, using absorption costing since it means the cost of sales will be lower.

Standard costing

7

7.1 Definition

Standard costing involves working out budgeted costs and budgeted sales for production. These are then compared against the actual figures so that managers can control costs and improve efficiency.

7.2 Advantages/benefits

Aid to planning - managers are forced to think ahead and plan for raw material and labour requirements.
Helps with motivation – it gives managers and workers something to aim at and helps to motivate them.
Creates an atmosphere of cost consciousness – therefore cuts waste and keeps down costs.
Improves efficiency – managers can see where there have been problems and therefore helps to improve efficiency.
Helps in determining selling prices - standard costs can be used to work out final selling prices.

7.3 Disadvantages/problems

Unforeseen raw material price increases – supplier prices can change quickly.
Unforeseen wage increases - e.g. overtime, union negotiates a better deal.
Competition – competitors might launch rival products or reduce prices therefore management price the product incorrectly.
Hidden costs – transport costs or exchange rate fluctuations.

7.4 Factors to take into account when determining standard costs

Regular monitoring and amendment of standards - standards need to be monitored regularly otherwise they will go out of date.
Make allowances for hidden costs – e.g. theft or waste of raw materials
Use work measurement techniques to establish standards – this way standards will be more accurate.
Production system should be fully planned before standards agreed – this way standards will be more accurate.

Standard costing

7.5 Types of variances

(i) Sales variances

- Total sales variance
- Sales price
- Sales volume variance

(ii) Materials variances

- Total materials variance
- Materials price variance
- Materials volume variance

(iii) Labour variances

- Total labour variance
- Labour rate variance
- Labour efficiency variance

In each case the total variance will be equal to the sum of the price and the volume variances.

7.6 Formulae

There are three formulae you need to know:

- Total variance = (SQ x SP) - (AQ x AP)
- Price/rate = (SP - AP) x AQ
- Volume/usage/efficiency = (SQ - AQ) x SP

7.7 Flexing the budget

This means adjusting the standard volumes of raw materials and labour (either up or down) for actual output. This is because the standard volumes of raw materials and labour have been based on budgeted output not actual output. If you don't flex the budget the standard volumes of raw material and labour won't be comparable to the actual volumes of raw materials and labour.

You never flex the sales figures.

7.8 Causes of variances

(i) Material usage variance – adverse

- Poor materials
- Poor machinery
- Poorly trained workers
- Poor management of workers

Reverse these for favourable variance.

(ii) Material price variance – adverse

- Better quality material used
- Supplier increased price
- General price inflation
- Change in quantity bought – therefore lost discount

Reverse these for favourable variance.

(iii) Labour efficiency variance – favourable

- Higher grade of labour used
- Better machinery used – investment
- Better management of workers
- Good working conditions, e.g. pay, physical environment – therefore better morale

Reverse these for adverse variance.

(iv) Labour rate variance – adverse

- Higher grade of skilled labour used
- Wage inflation
- Unions negotiated favourable pay deal
- Overtime rates paid

Reverse these for favourable variance.

(v) Sales price variance – adverse

- Competition

Standard costing

- Price reductions to attract new market segment or new customers
- End of year sales

Reverse these for favourable variance.

(vi) Sales volume variance – adverse

- Competition
- Change in consumer tastes
- Higher price
- Poor quality product
- Poor marketing – branding, advertising

Reverse these for favourable variance.

7.9 Reconciliation statements

You should be able to reconcile the budgeted and actual figures for these three items:

- Profits
- Costs
- Sales

See appendix 4 for formats.

Capital investment appraisal

8

8.1 Definition

Investment appraisal is a set of techniques used to determine whether a capital investment project should go ahead. It's also used to rank projects in order of desirability.

8.2 Reasons for investment

- To replace worn out non-current assets
- To stay competitive - other businesses may be updating their non-current assets, so you have to do the same.
- Availability and development of new technology – e.g. computer aided manufacture.
- To reduce costs
- Expectations of future growth and profits – business may be in a growing market so it wants to increase productivity.

8.3 Methods of appraisal

There are two methods you need to know for the syllabus - payback period and net present value (NPV).

(i) Payback period

This measures the amount of time it takes a firm to recoup its initial investment.

Worked example

XYZ Ltd wants to invest £400,000 in new machinery. Calculate the payback period for this investment given the following forecast cash flows:

Year 1	Year 2	Year 3	Year 4	Year 5
£	£	£	£	£
100,000	125,000	125,000	100,000	100,000

Solution

Payback = 3yrs + (50,000 ÷ 100,000) x 365 days

Investment appraisal

= 3 yrs 182 days

Advantages

- Simple to operate and easy to understand
- Useful for firms with difficult cash flow positions as it helps them identify how long it will take to get their money back
- Focuses on the short-term, so less likely to be inaccurate - the further you project figures ahead the more inaccurate your data is likely to be.

Disadvantages

- Ignores profitability, just focuses on cash flow.
- Ignores time value of money - doesn't take into account inflation
- Ignores timing and size of cash flows
- Ignores receipts after the payback period - these may be significant
- Ignores scrap values - these may be significant
- May encourage short-termism - may be a tendency to choose a project that gives the quickest payback and ignore returns.

(ii) Net present value (NPV)

The NPV of an investment is the value today of the estimated cash flows in the future less the initial capital cost. Each year's cash flow is multiplied by a 'discount factor' to re-state it in today's terms. The project with the highest NPV is the one you should recommend. Projects with negative NPV's should be rejected. You will always be given a discount table of the discount factor you should use.

Worked example

XYZ Ltd wants to invest £500,000 in new plant and machinery. Calculate its NPV if the cost of capital is 10% and the cash flows are as follows:

	Year 1	Year 2	Year 3	Year 4	Year 5
		£	£	£	£	£
Cash flow		100,000	125,000	125,000	150,000	180,000
Discount factor		0.909	0.826	0.751	0.683	0.621
Discounted cash flow		90,900	103,250	93,875	102,450	111,780

Total DCF's = £502,255

Investment appraisal

Less: Capital cost = (£500,000)
NPV = +£2,555

Advantages

- Takes into account the time value of money
- Takes into account all receipts and scrap values

Disadvantages

- More difficult to understand for the non-specialist
- Depends on accuracy of predictions
- Difficult to select discount factor - good projects may get rejected

8.4 Qualitative factors/non-financial factors to take into account when making investment decisions

Comparing like-with-like - e.g. choosing between two types of plant and machinery is not just as simple as looking at cash flow. The firm also has to consider quality, performance, safety, and maintenance costs.
Competitor's behavior - competitors may have recently updated their plant and machinery, so you may have to do the same.
External factors - e.g. state of the economy, exchange rates, interest rates, inflation.
Social factors - e.g. environmental impact, pollution, redundancies and effect on the local community.
Capacity – ability of investment to cope with a growing market.
Scrap values – these may be significant.
Order levels - are they high or low, increasing or decreasing? Do the order levels justify the investment?
Use of estimates – how reliable are the figures you are using? Also, the longer you forecast ahead the less likely the figures are to be accurate.
Confidence - how confident are the managers the project will succeed.

Social accounting

9

Social accounting is the non-financial factors which businesses have to take into account when making business decisions. The questions will probably focus on the effects on these three groups:

- Shareholders
- Employees
- Local community

Examples

- Closure of an unprofitable factory in a deprived area
- Replacement of labour by new technology
- Redundancies and cost cutting
- Use of non-renewable energy
- Chemical plant opening up in a rural area

9.1 General points to think about

Shareholders

- Effects on dividends, profits and share price
- Effect on image and reputation of the business

Employees

- Effect on job security
- Effect on morale and productivity
- How trade unions may react
- Effect on health and safety

Local community

- Effect on local economy, e.g. local reverse multiplier effect
- Jobs
- Pollution and environmental damage
- Health risks
- Effect on house prices

Activity Based Costing (ABC)

10

10.1 Definition

This is an alternative to absorption costing, and uses activity levels in different departments and stages of the production process to allocate overheads, rather than overhead absorption rates such as machine hours and labour hours.

10.2 Cost pool

This a group of overhead costs incurred by the same activity, e.g., purchasing costs for goods would include several overhead costs – wages of purchasing staff, light/heat/rent of running purchasing office and telephone/post/email relating to purchasing. All of these would be grouped into a 'cost pool'.

10.3 Cost driver

These are the activities that cause costs to be incurred, e.g.

Activity	Cost driver
Processing orders to suppliers	Number of orders
Processing invoices received from suppliers	Number of invoices
Factory canteen expenses	Number of employees
Factory machine expenses	Machine hours

10.4 Benefits/Drawbacks of ABC

Benefits

- Should be more accurate than absorption costing as its using activity levels in different departments/stages of production process to allocate overheads rather than arbitrary measures such as labour hours and machine hours which may not be relevant, e.g. machine hours for administration costs.
- Final selling prices will be calculated more accurately as they are based on a more realistic full cost price

Activity based costing

- It charges each product with the use of an activity, so costs can be controlled i.e. reduce the activity and therefore reduce costs and increase profits
- It considers that batch sizes affect costs. This is ignored in absorption costing as a small batch may have expensive set up costs
- Acceptable under IAS 2, inventories

Drawbacks

- More complicated than absorption costing as there are more cost pools and cost drivers involved in the calculations. Therefore it takes longer and is more difficult for the non-specialist to understand
- Cost pools may have more than one cost driver, e.g. marketing costs are driven by both the number of staff hours and number of marketing campaigns. Therefore decisions still have to be made on which one to use.
- Cost drivers and cost pools need to be kept up to date to remain relevant

APPENDIX 1 – Manufacturing & Income statement layout and extract from Balance Sheet

(i) Manufacturing & Income statement for XYZ Ltd for the year ended 31 December 20XX

	£	£
Direct materials		
Opening inventory of raw materials	X	
Add: Purchases of raw materials	X	
Less: Closing inventory of raw materials	(X)	X
Direct labour		X
Direct expenses		
Royalties		X
Prime Cost		X
Factory overheads		
Light & heat	X	
Power	X	
Depreciation – plant & machinery	X	
Indirect wages	X	
Insurance	X	
Maintenance	X	X
Work-in-progress adjustment		
Opening W-I-P	X	
Closing W-I-P	(X)	X/(X)
Costs of completed production		X
Add: Manufacturing profit		X
Transfer price of finished goods		X
Revenue (revenue – returns in)		X
Cost of sales		
Opening inventory of finished goods	X	
Add: Transfer price of finished goods	X	
Less: Closing inventory of finished goods	(X)	(X)
Gross profit		X
Manufacturing profit		X
Increase/Decrease in PURP		(X)/X

Expenses

Rent & rates	X	
Insurance	X	
Administration expenses	X	
Director's salaries	X	
Office salaries	X	
Depreciation – office equipment	X	(X)
Profit for year		X

(ii) Extract from balance sheet for XYZ Ltd as at 31 December 20XX

	£	£
Current assets		
Inventory - raw materials	X	
- W-I-P	X	
- finished goods	X	
Less: PURP	(X)	X

APPENDIX 2 - Budget Layouts

(i) Production budget (units)

	J	F	M	A	M	J
Units						
Sales	X	X	X	X	X	X
Opening stock	(X)	(X)	(X)	(X)	(X)	(X)
Closing stock	X	X	X	X	X	X
Production (units)	X	X	X	X	X	X

(ii) Purchases

	J	F	M	A	M	J
Units						
Sales	X	X	X	X	X	X
Opening stock	(X)	(X)	(X)	(X)	(X)	(X)
Closing stock	X	X	X	X	X	X
Purchases (units)	X	X	X	X	X	X
Purchases cost	£X	£X	£X	£X	£X	£X

(iii) Receivables budget

	J	F	M	A	M	J
	£	£	£	£	£	£
b/f	X	X	X	X	X	X
Credit sales	X	X	X	X	X	X
Receipts from debtors	(X)	(X)	(X)	(X)	(X)	(X)
Discounts allowed	(X)	(X)	(X)	(X)	(X)	(X)
Bad debts	(X)	(X)	(X)	(X)	(X)	(X)
c/f	X	X	X	X	X	X

(iv) Payables budget

	J	F	M	A	M	J
	£	£	£	£	£	£
b/f	X	X	X	X	X	X
Credit purchases	X	X	X	X	X	X
Payments to creditors	(X)	(X)	(X)	(X)	(X)	(X)
Discounts received	(X)	(X)	(X)	(X)	(X)	(X)
c/f	X	X	X	X	X	X

(v) Labour budget

	J	F	M	A	M	J
Labour hours	X	X	X	X	X	X
Labour cost	£X	£X	£X	£X	£X	£X

(vi) Sales budget

	J	F	M	A	M	J
Sales units	X	X	X	X	X	X
Sales value	£X	£X	£X	£X	£X	£X

APPENDIX 3 - Marginal cost statement

	£
Revenue	X
Variable costs	(X)
Total contribution	X
Fixed costs	(X)
Profit for year	X

APPENDIX 4 – Standard Costing Reconciliation Statements

(i) Profit reconciliation

			£
Budgeted profit			X
Flexed profit			X

Adjustments	ADV	FAV	
Sales price	X		
Material price		X	
Material usage	X		
Labour rate	X		
Labour efficiency		X	
	(X)	X	(X)/X

Actual profit — X

(ii) Cost reconciliation

			£
Budgeted cost			X

Adjustments	ADV	FAV	
Material price		X	
Material usage	X		
Labour rate	X		
Labour efficiency		X	
	X	(X)	X/(X)*

Actual cost — X

*Favourable variances reduce costs but adverse variances increase costs.

(iii) Sales reconciliation

			£
Budgeted sales			X

Adjustments	ADV	FAV	
Sales price	X		
Sales volume		X	
	(X)	X	(X)/X

Actual sales — X

Index

A

absorption costing, 20-23
activity based costing, 32-33
allocation, 21
apportionment, 21, 22

B

break-even analysis, 12-14
break-even point, 12, 13, 15
budgetary control, 5
budgeting, 5-9

C

cash budget, 5, 6, 7
contribution, 10, 11, 15, 16, 17
cost driver, 32
cost pool, 32

D

direct costs, 10

F

fixed costs, 10, 20
flexing the budget, 25

I

indirect costs, 10
investment appraisal, 28-30

L

labour budget, 5, 7
labour efficiency variance, 25, 26
labour rate variance, 25, 26

M

make or buy decisions, 15, 16
manufacturing accounts, 3-4
marginal costing, 10, 15-19
marginal costs, 10
master budget, 5, 8
material price variance, 26
material usage variance, 26

N

net present value, 29

O

optimum use of scarce resources, 15, 17
overhead absorption rates, 20, 32

P

payback period, 28
production budget, 5, 7
provision for unrealised profit, 4

S

sales budget, 5, 7
sales price variance, 26
sales volume variance, 25, 27
social accounting, 31
special orders, 15
standard costing, 24-27

T

target rate of profit, 13
transfer pricing, 3, 4

Index

types of variances, 25

V

variable costs, 10

W

work-in-progress, 3

Printed in Great Britain
by Amazon